ENERGY DRINK

Strength for Today and Solutions for Tomorrow

Calories: LOVE

KAKRA BAIDEN

DEDICATION

I dedicate this devotional to Brian Adu.

IN THE MIDST OF THE STORM

Peace I leave with you, my peace I give unto
you: not as the world giveth, give I unto you.
Let not your heart be troubled,
neither let it be afraid.

—JOHN 14:27

Peace is a very important element in our lives. We all need peace in our marriages, businesses, homes, and offices, among others. One of the reasons why Jesus came into the world is to bring peace. He said, "Peace, I leave with you." The peace Jesus brings is not of this world. The peace of this world is based on circumstances and conditions.

Some years ago I was on a plane travelling. During the flight we heard a loud noise emanating from the engine of the plane. We could tell there was something wrong. Suddenly people started to panic. For some strange reason, I kept calm. One woman turned to me and asked, "Are you not afraid?" I answered and said, "I am not because we cannot die." She turned to a section of the passengers and said, "There is a man here who says we will not die." Suddenly they gathered around me and asked, "Is it true that we will not die?" I replied, "Yes!" I was calm in the midst of the chaos. Why? Because the peace of God is a person called the Holy Spirit.

David, in the midst of all his adversaries, enjoyed peace. He said in Psalm 4:8, "I will both lay me down in peace, and sleep: for thou, LORD, only makest me dwell in safety." It is based on relationship, not circumstances.

As a matter of fact, you can be married and suffer from insecurity although everything may be normal. However, you can be calm and happy in the midst of chaos.

> ...The LORD [is] my light and my salvation; whom shall I fear? the LORD [is] the strength of my life; of whom shall I be afraid? —PSALM 27:1

That is the kind of peace God brings.

This year, may you experience peace in your marriage, business, and heart, in the name of Jesus! Cultivate a relationship with the Holy Spirit and experience the peace of God!

DECISION-MAKING PROCESS

Butter and honey shall he eat, that he may
know to refuse the evil, and choose the good.
—ISAIAH 7:15

We all make countless minor and major decisions on a daily basis. Even the minor ones aggregate over time to become major decisions. For example, simple decisions concerning what you eat and drink eventually determine your health and wealth. Major decisions like marriage can leave a bitter or sweet taste in your mouth for the rest of your life.

To make good decisions, you must first know "how to refuse the evil, and choose the good." This means discernment. All that glitters is not gold; it could be the eye of a snake.

Secondly, you must have the strength or will to choose good. When it comes to matters of love, passion can overpower good judgement.

The solution is to eat "butter and honey," i.e., the Word of God. It will increase your discernment and strengthen your will. Butter is a product of milk, and we are told in 1 Peter 2:2 that the Word is like milk.

In Ezekiel 3:3, the prophet said the Word became like honey in his mouth.

Read the Word daily to help you make good decisions!

BODY LANGUAGE

A servant will not be corrected by words: for
though he understand he will not answer.
— PROVERBS 29:19

Body language is nonverbal communication consisting of gestures, body posture, eye movements, and facial expressions. I think women communicate more through body language than men. I can take one look at my wife's face or posture and know what she is saying to me. I have been married to her for many years, so I can read her.

Men will have to learn the body language of women to be able to relate with them properly because most of their concerns may not be expressed verbally.

What does it mean when you ask someone a question and the person refuses to answer? I want to share with you one body language tip from the Scriptures.

When you ask someone a question and he or she does not reply, the Bible says it means the person cannot be corrected by words. In other words, they are unrepentant.

I once got angry with someone I used to employ because he had done something wrong. I did not receive even one answer from him as I questioned him about what he had done.

Watch husbands, wives, employees, children, and people who answer serious questions with stony silence. It means they are unrepentant and will not change. Try something else; maybe prayer, dismissal, or counselling from another person!

FATAL ATTRACTION

Hell and destruction are never full; so the eyes
of man are never satisfied.

— PROVERBS 27:20

Any time I read the story of Samson and Delilah,
I get fascinated by how Delilah was able to
get Samson to tell her the secret of his strength. It
was clear to Samson that Delilah wanted to kill him
because she had made previous attempts to do so.
Finally, she succeeded! It was a fatal attraction!

In summary, I can say Samson was charmed to
destruction and death. The word "charm" means
compelling attractiveness. She was an attractive
woman. Why is it that we can sometimes walk
knowingly towards death and destruction even
when we are aware of the consequences?

Why keep a relationship that is destroying you?
Why take a decision that you know will end your
career or destroy your family? Why keep friends
who are destroying you?

You can always charm human beings by showing
them something which looks attractive and beautiful and they will sometimes follow irrespective
of the consequences. Because our eyes are never
satisfied, they can be charmed. A beautiful woman,
handsome man, money, or a glorious opportunity
can charm you to your death. All that glitters is not
gold; it could be the eye of a snake.

Be guided by the Word, not your eyes, for we walk
by faith not by sight!

NOT EASILY OFFENDED

Great peace have they which love thy law:
and nothing shall offend them.
— PSALM 119:165

Are you easily offended or short-tempered? If you are, it will be difficult for you to maintain long-term relationships because as long as you are close to people, someone is bound to step on your toe.

If you are married, it may be difficult to sustain a prolonged conversation with your spouse without trouble because some misplaced word can easily pierce your fragile emotions.

I believe if you are in such a situation you will need some form of emotional healing and strength. Scripture says, take no heed to all words that are spoken, else you will hear your servant curse you. In other words, don't be easily offended.

What can you do to avoid offence? By loving the Word of God. When we read and meditate on the Word, it can have two positive effects on us.

Firstly, we shall experience great peace, because God will become the source of our peace, not circumstances.

Secondly, we shall not be easily offended. Why is this so? Because the Word acts like a shock absorber to your soul; it helps you to absorb the painful and hurtful words of others. Read it and obey it and you shall not be easily offended!

BORN OF GOD

Which were born, not of blood, nor of the will
of the flesh, nor of the will of man, but of God.
—JOHN 1:13

The word "birth" can be defined as initiating
something or creating something. An idea or
company can be birthed by someone. There are
several means by which an individual can give
birth to something.

We learn from this verse that birthing can come in
three forms: by blood, the will of the flesh, and the
will of God.

1. You can give birth to something by blood or
    natural means.

2. You can give birth to something by your
    will. Your "will" is your power of choice.

3. You can give birth to something by following
    the will of God. This means using biblical
    principles and the Word of God and letting
    God take the initiative.

The best way to birth anything, be it a business,
ministry, family, or idea, is by following the will of
God. This is because the will of God is enduring,
"Whosoever doeth the will of God abides forever."
The will of God is invincible, "Whatsoever is born
of God overcomes the world."

Let God birth your dreams. Surrender to His will
by obeying His Word!

ENVY

They envied Moses also in the camp,
and Aaron the saint of the LORD.
— PSALM 106:16

One of the signs of envy is criticism. Sometimes people who criticize us are actually envious of us. Moses and Aaron came under heavy criticism from Korah and the two hundred and fifty princes of Israel; they accused Moses of marrying an Ethiopian woman and pride.

Pride is an accusation that is difficult to fight because of its nebulous nature. On the outside Moses' critics looked righteous and zealous for God. But deep down in their hearts they were envious.

In God's sight Moses and Aaron were saints; blameless.

Sometimes in an office environment people can pick on your little flaws and human frailties. Sometimes friends, colleagues, peers, the press, and classmates can criticize every single thing you do.

Don't be worried, because it's a sign that you are blessed! Blessings birth envy, envy births criticism, and your critics are a badge and proof that you are blessed!

HOW TO OVERCOME THE DEVIL

And they overcame him by the blood of the
Lamb, and by the word of their testimony;
and they loved not their lives unto the death.
—REVELATION 12:11

The three key assignments of the devil are to steal, kill, and destroy.

Recently I was praying for someone who was afflicted by evil spirits. The spirits made the person move like a snake on the floor, screaming and shouting. The poor soul was being tormented! By prayer I overcame the devil, and the person was set free.

Three things helped me to do this:

1. **The blood of the Lamb.** I said, "By the blood of the Lamb, I command you to come out!" Our mouth is the brush, or hyssop, which we use to apply the blood in the realm of the spirit. As I said this, the blood was released.

2. **The word of my testimony.** I had to confess the Word of God to release the power in it.

3. **Boldness.** It takes boldness to tackle the devil. "You must not love your life to the death." This implies boldness. In a sense, you must not be afraid to die.

Fear keeps many from confronting demons. If you are afraid, demons can sense it. Now, step into the ring with boldness, and take the devil out!

PEER PRESSURE

Nevertheless the people refused to obey the
voice of Samuel; and they said, Nay; but we
will have a king over us; that we also may be
like all the nations; and that our king may judge
us, and go out before us, and fight our battles.
—1 SAMUEL 8:19-20

The word "peer" means one that is of equal
standing with another: equal; one belonging to
the same societal group, especially based on age,
grade, or status.

Your peers can exert an invisible pressure on you
to make you want to be like them. Everyone in the
office is buying a new car so you feel obliged to buy
one, although you cannot afford it. Everyone in
your family may be going for a holiday so you may
want to go too, although you cannot afford it. Peer
pressure can afflict an individual, family, child, the
old, and even a nation.

Israel succumbed to peer pressure and demanded
for a king because they wanted to be like all the
other nations. In the end it was not a blessing to
them.

It is always important to listen to the Lord instead
of yielding to peer pressure because the leading of
the Lord is the highest form of wisdom!

UAVS (FIGHTING FROM HEAVEN)

Zebulun and Naphtali were a people that
jeoparded their lives unto the death . . . then
fought the kings of Canaan . . . they took
no gain of money.
— JUDGES 5:18-20

Modern warfare has changed dramatically from infantry soldiers fighting on foot to UAVs, the acronym for "unmanned aerial vehicles." These are tiny computerized unmanned planes equipped with cameras and ammunition. They can kill enemy targets from the sky. They can remain hidden in the skies for hours, monitoring enemy movements.

Modern warfare is conducted from the sky. Scripture tells us we are in a spiritual war and we must conduct the war from heaven, not with carnal or physical tools like relying on men. They fought from heaven; the stars in their courses fought against Sisera. Sisera was the army commander of Jabin, king of Caanan, who had a mighty army. Zebulun and Naphtali managed to defeat him with a smaller army. They did not accomplish this through "the gain of money."

There are many Christians who rely on money to fight their battles of sickness, poverty, marriage, promotion, etc. If you don't have any money, what are you going to do? They fought from heaven; they used heavenly weapons like "faith" and "prayer." I remember recently commanding someone to come out of a coma and the person came out. Faith is a UAV that can spiritually help you win the wars in your home and office. Use it and learn to fight from heaven!

GRACE AND THE ASSIGNMENT

And Moses said unto Hobab, the son of Raguel
the Midianite, Moses' father in law, We are
journeying unto the place of which the LORD
said, I will give it you: come thou with us, and
we will do thee good: for the LORD hath spoken
good concerning Israel.

—NUMBERS 10:29

How can you tap into the grace of God? I believe there are several ways, but I want to show you one of them.

The grace of God can be found in the assignment or plan of God. Moses asked his brother in-law, Hobab, to journey with them to the land of Canaan. He assured him by saying, "We will do thee good."

Why was he so assured? Because he knew the plan they were following was not a man-made plan, but a plan from God. God finances and provides for His plans. Moses said, "The Lord has spoken good concerning Israel."

When you come across someone who has an assignment from God, you can easily tap into the grace of God by tapping into the plan. The grace may not be on the man, but on the assignment.

For example, I have been mandated by the Lord to teach the nations with signs through radio, TV, the Internet, and conferences. I have seen many people blessed without measure as they have helped me to carry out this mandate. They become partakers of the grace that is on the assignment.

May you tap into the grace of God on your assignment!

HOW TO DEAL WITH CONFUSION

For the Lord GOD will help me; therefore shall I
not be confounded: therefore have I set my face
like a flint, and I know that I shall
not be ashamed.

—ISAIAH 50:7

I don't know about you, but there have been instances in my life where I have been confounded or confused. "Confusion" means to be disturbed in the mind.

Have you ever been confused before? You did not know whether to marry George or Felix; you did not know whether to work for company A or B; you did not know whether to enter into full-time ministry or not; amongst many others. Here is something you can do to overcome confusion or being confounded.

You can escape confusion if you seek the help of God.

If it's a decision, you can pray that the will of God be done. That's what Jesus did.

If it's about protection from your enemies in your office, you can pray and be rest assured by faith that He will protect you.

If it's a crisis, you can pray that God provides for you.

Prayer enlists the help of God. Keep on praying!

STOP WHINING. IT'S DANGEROUS!

> And the people spake against God, and against
> Moses, Wherefore have ye brought us up out
> of Egypt to die in the wilderness? for there is
> no bread, neither is there any water; and our
> soul loatheth this light bread. And the LORD sent
> fiery serpents among the people, and they bit
> the people; and much people of Israel died.
> —NUMBERS 21:5-6

It is important to know the nature of the people in your life so you can know how to interact with them effectively. For example, in an office situation you must know what your boss hates and avoid these things. What you think is important may not be important to him.

When Israel built the golden calf, God was angry with them, but He did not tell them they would not enter the Promised Land. When they murmured and the twelve spies brought the evil report, God said they would not enter the Promised Land.

When Israel murmured against God concerning food, He allowed serpents to bite them to death. God hates murmuring and murmuring releases the serpent, "the devil."

I remember once murmuring and complaining about something. Later I had a vision and saw myself in prison being guarded by demons. I had opened the door for the serpent. I pleaded with God, and out of mercy I was released. Stop murmuring, for God hates it!

THE PRIEST AND THE CANDLESTICK

Speak unto Aaron, and say unto him, When
thou lightest the lamps, the seven lamps shall
give light over against the candlestick.
—NUMBERS 8:2

The Old Testament is full of symbols, which
have a bearing on us. This verse contains an
instruction God gave to Aaron concerning priestly
service. I want us to consider two things:

1. The priest was supposed to light the lamps.
2. The purpose was for the lamps to give light.

What does this symbolize? In the book of Revelation
Jesus gave an interpretation of the candlesticks. He
said they represented the church.

. . . the seven candlesticks which thou sawest are
the seven churches.   —REVELATION 1:20

Therefore, we as members of the church are
supposed to shine or give light. What kind of light
is this? It is the light of "good works."

Jesus said in Matthew 5:16, "Let your light so shine
before men, that they may see your good works,
and glorify your Father which is in heaven."

The responsibility of Aaron was to light the candlestick, or church. Fire is needed to set the church
ablaze, and the preaching of God's Word by His
ministers sets the candlestick, or church, on fire.

. . . But his word was in mine heart as a burning
fire.   —JEREMIAH 20:9

Attend church every Sunday to light your candlestick, and make sure you glow with good works!

HOW TO PLEASE GOD

Will the LORD be pleased with thousands of
rams, or with ten thousands of rivers of oil?
He hath shewed thee, O man, what is good;
and what doth the LORD require of thee,
but to do justly, and to love mercy,
and to walk humbly with thy God?

— MICAH 6:7-8

During the baptism of Jesus, the heavens were
opened and a voice said, "This is my beloved
Son, in whom I am well pleased." What did He
do to win the pleasure of the Lord? It could not be
ministry, because He was not as yet in ministry; it
could not be the cross, because He had not gone to
the cross. What are some of the things that please
the Lord and win His favour? Three things are
mentioned which please God.

First of all, to do justly. The original meaning of that
word is "judgment." We must judge things the way
God judges. For example, we must adopt God's
standards and values. Did you know God values
obedience more than money?

Secondly, to love mercy. This means actively
showing mercy to the weak, the poor, and the
vulnerable, and not taking advantage of them.

Finally, to walk humbly with God. This means to
be obedient and follow the Lord wherever He will
lead us through His Word and Spirit. Please God by
doing these!

DON'T FIGHT YOUR OWN PRAYER

And God saw their works, that they turned
from their evil way; and God repented of the
evil, that he had said that he would do unto
them; and he did it not.

—JONAH 3:10

I have come across people who have prayed,
fasted, and cried to the Lord for their prayers to
be answered. Sometimes, instead of being thankful,
these same people become angry with the Lord
when their requests are granted.

Jonah was sent to Nineveh to preach the Gospel.
The people repented after hearing his message, so
God forgave them.

This was Jonah's reaction.

But it displeased Jonah exceedingly, and he was
very angry.

—JONAH 4:1

I once prayed with someone for her husband to
stop cheating on her. Later the man broke up this
relationship and returned to his wife. His wife,
who had prayed for his return, was now angry and
unwilling to accept him back.

I have seen people pray for a husband and after the
marriage fight that same husband till he leaves the
home. I have also seen people pray desperately for
a job and later complain bitterly about the same job.

Instead of fighting our prayers, let's be thankful to
God for answered prayer!

DON'T BE DEFINED BY BAD
EXPERIENCES

And the angel of the Lord appeared unto him,
and said unto him, The Lord is with thee, thou
mighty man of valour. And Gideon said unto
him, Oh my Lord, if the Lord be with us, why
then is all this befallen us? and where be all his
miracles which our fathers told us of, saying,
Did not the Lord bring us up from Egypt? but
now the Lord hath forsaken us, and delivered
us into the hands of the Midianites.
—JUDGES 6:12-13

There are many people who allow one bad experience to define or determine the rest of their
lives. The fact that you are divorced, failed an exam,
or got pregnant out of wedlock does not mean you
are a failure. The fact that you are in a garage does
not mean you are a car. God does not define you by
your experiences; neither should you.

God saw Gideon as a mighty man, but he saw
himself through the mirror of his then experience: a
poor and oppressed Israelite.

Someone once told me her life was over because
her boyfriend had left her. I told her, "You can love
again. There are billions of better men out there."

You are who God says you are, and not what your
experiences say you are!

BLUEPRINT FOR YOUR LIFE

Who serve unto the example and shadow of
heavenly things, as Moses was admonished
of God when he was about to make the
tabernacle: for See, saith he, that thou
make all things according to the pattern
shewed to thee in the mount.

—HEBREWS 8:5

The term "blueprint" is used to describe the printed plan of a building. The blueprint of a building is supposed to be the same as the building after it is built. The building is a manifestation of the plan.

Every life has a blueprint in heaven. The life you lead on earth is supposed to reflect the plan that God has for your life. God gave Moses a vision to build a temple on earth, and it had to conform to the plan in heaven.

Nowadays God is building a spiritual temple, which is you. When you die, will the life you lead on earth conform to the plan that God has for you? God will compare the life you led with the plan He had for you.

Did you marry who God wanted you to marry? Did you live where He wanted you to live? Did you use your time the way He wanted you to use it?

Let us live a life based on the plan that God drew for us from eternity, and we will lead a life pleasing to Him!

BEWARE OF HASTY DECISIONS

And Satan stood up against Israel, and
provoked David to number Israel.
—1 CHRONICLES 21:1

There are certain actions that we take that are instigated by the devil. Sometimes a rash business decision can destroy years of hard work.

I once knew a gentleman. One day he decided to break his relationship with the girl he loved. He later rescinded his decision, but it was too late; the girl left him.

What makes us sometimes take rash and hasty decisions to our destruction?

Some people can suddenly resign from a good job for no good reason and live with the regret of unemployment for years. Church members can suddenly leave a good church for no reason. What happened? They were provoked by the devil.

The original Hebrew definition of that word is to prick or stimulate. Some of these rash and sudden decisions are orchestrated by the devil.

Next time you are being tempted to make a rash decision, to make a major decision about a temporary situation, or to focus on the minor and major on the minor, remember that maybe you are being provoked by the devil.

You need to be patient, prayerful, and study the Word, and it won't be long, that rash decision will be discarded!

BITTERSWEET MEDICINE

And I went unto the angel, and said unto him,
Give me the little book. And he said unto me,
Take it, and eat it up; and it shall make
thy belly bitter, but it shall be in
thy mouth sweet as honey.
—REVELATION 10:9

In Revelation 10:9, John describes the effect of the Word of God on our lives. I wonder why many medicines are bitter. The thing which is supposed to cure us is often bitter and difficult to swallow, yet the same bitter pill is supposed to bring relief and joy.

God's Word is like that; it is bittersweet. There are many people with sick bodies, relationships, marriages, character, spirits, and finances. The way out is the medicine of God's Word.

To take the bitterness of a failed relationship, demonic oppression, or a difficult past out of your life, you will have to first embrace the bitterness of God's Word. You may have to make some sacrifices, but remember that most medicines are bitter to taste, but bring relief at the end.

God's Word is like that. Open your heart and receive it, because afterwards it shall be as honey in your mouth.

Take it by obeying it!

ABOVE THE LAW

[This] I say then, Walk in the Spirit, and ye
shall not fulfil the lust of the flesh. For the flesh
lusteth against the Spirit, and the Spirit against
the flesh: and these are contrary the one to the
other: so that ye cannot do the things that ye
would. But if ye be led of the Spirit, ye are not
under the law.

—GALATIANS 5:16-18

There is a constant war between your flesh and
your spirit for the control of your life, and the
dominant one will win. The word "lusteth" means
to fight. When the Holy Spirit controls your life,
you will not have to be guided by rules because He
will influence you to do the right things.

If you have a husband who is full of the Spirit, you
will not have to make laws to make him love you
and be faithful to you because the Holy Spirit will
influence him to do it.

If he is not ruled by the Spirit, you may want to
make rules to control him. You may want to insist
that he comes home at a certain time, check his text
messages and e-mails to monitor him, and ask him
not to talk to some particular women, etc.

However, a man who is led by the Spirit will live
above the law.

Let us decide to be influenced by the Holy Spirit
and we will live above human laws!

ADD TO YOUR FAITH

And beside this, giving all diligence, add to
your faith virtue; and to virtue knowledge.
For if these things be in you, and abound,
they make you that ye shall neither
be barren nor unfruitful in the knowledge
of our Lord Jesus Christ.

— 2 PETER 1:5, 8

Why is it that although some people become born again, it does not seem to reflect on their lives spiritually, economically, martially, or socially?

Every product that exists in a raw form will have little value until value is added to it. For example, cooked rice has a higher value than raw rice because value has been added to it.

There are people who assume that because they have given their lives to Christ by faith, it automatically qualifies them to be successful at anything.

I remember when I was in high school. There were Christians who did not study much because they felt being Christians entitled them to success during exams. Many of them failed woefully. They forgot to add other important qualities like discipline and knowledge to their faith in God. The result was a barren and unfruitful Christian life.

Faith in God is the first step to a more fulfilling life. Do not forget to add other qualities that will make you all that God wants you to be. Decide to be a more fruitful Christian by adding to your faith!

DO YOU WANT TO HEAR GOD'S VOICE?

My sheep hear my voice, and I know them,
and they follow me:
—JOHN 10:27

Do you want to hear God's voice? I guess we all do. The ability to hear God's voice is crucial if you want God to bless you.

I remember once travelling on a highway at top speed. In the middle of my journey I heard God say, "Stop." I wondered why. I pulled off the road and parked. I got out and walked round the car and all seemed to be well. Suddenly I heard a loud explosion; one of my tires exploded. The Lord had delivered me from a potential major accident. You may ask, "How can I also hear God's voice?"

To hear God's voice, you must be a sheep. When you become a sheep, God will open your spiritual ears. Goats cannot hear God's voice.

How can you be a sheep? Jesus said, "They follow me." Sheep don't follow their ideas, feelings, emotions, circumstances, religion, or the world.

Determine to follow the "logos" or written Word of God. It will not be long; you will be hearing the "rhema" or spoken Word of God!

COLLATERAL DAMAGE

And Saul said unto the Kenites, Go, depart, get
you down from among the Amalekites, lest I
destroy you with them: for ye shewed kindness
to all the children of Israel, when they came
up out of Egypt. So the Kenites departed from
among the Amalekites.

—1 SAMUEL 15:6

Collateral damage is injury inflicted on something other than an intended target. As
Christians, we are warned not to be unnecessarily
close to unbelievers. One Scripture is, "Be ye not
unequally yoked together with unbelievers"
(2 Cor. 6:14). For example, a Christian is not
supposed to marry an unbeliever even if he or she
is drowning in love. Why is this so?

God instructed Saul to destroy the Amalekites
because they had been hostile to the Israelites.
One way God executes judgment is by using other
people as instruments of judgment.

The Kenites, another tribe that had been kind to
Israel, were friends with the Amalekites and were
living amongst them. Saul advised them to separate themselves, otherwise they would also be
destroyed and be victims of collateral damage.

Unbelievers can easily attract the judgment of God
because of their rebellion. A certain close association with them can make us victims of collateral
damage in the day God executes His judgment.
Do you want to avoid collateral damage? Be ye not
unequally yoked together with unbelievers!

CONFESSION AND DEMONS

And he said unto her, For this saying go thy
way; the devil is gone out of thy daughter.

—MARK 7:29

Did you know that confessions drive out demons? No wonder Scripture states, "They overcame him by the blood of the Lamb, and by the word of their testimony" (Rev. 12:11).

A woman expressed faith in Jesus by telling Him, "Even the children eat of the crumbs which fall from their master's table" (Mk. 7:28). She said she only needed a crumb of healing from Jesus. Jesus told her that her confession had made her child whole.

I want you to note that Jesus said it was the *confession* or saying of the woman that had made it possible for her daughter to be healed. Confession is the trigger that releases the power of God's Word.

Keep on confessing good things about yourself and watch demons flee!

CONTAGIOUS

And the officers shall speak further unto the
people, and they shall say, What man is there
that is fearful and fainthearted? let him go and
return unto his house, lest his brethren's heart
faint as well as his heart.

—DEUTERONOMY 20:8

The word "contagious" means something that is capable of being transmitted by bodily contact with an infected person or object.

Emotions can be contagious, so it's important to associate with people with the right emotions. An association with people with negative emotions like bitterness, anger, hopelessness, frustration, doubt, etc., can spread amongst a group of people who are closely related.

Moses urged Israel not to let people who were afraid go to war because negative emotions are contagious. He said, "Let him go and return unto his house, lest his brethren's heart faint as well as his heart."

Are you struggling with negative emotions? Check your friends! It may be time to separate yourself because you may be hanging out with the wrong group.

Hang out with Jesus by letting Him speak to you through His Word and you will turn into a lion, because He is the Lion of the Tribe of Judah!

DO YOU WANT TO LIVE LONG?

For thou, O God, hast heard my vows: thou
hast given me the heritage of those that fear thy
name. Thou wilt prolong the king's life: and his
years as many generations.

— PSALM 61:5-6

L ong life is a product of both physical and spiritual things. Spiritually there are things you can do to prolong your life, and this verse reveals one of the secrets. Let's examine it in detail.

The first thing I want you to notice is there are certain blessings that are our heritage or inheritance: "Thou hast given me the heritage."

Secondly, long life can be inherited from the Lord: "Thou wilt prolong the king's life."

Thirdly, one criterion for accessing this inheritance is "the fear of the Lord."

The fear of the Lord can help you live a long and healthy life.

Walk in obedience today because obedience is counted as the fear of the Lord!

FOUR REASONS WHY YOU MUST NOT BE AFRAID OF MAN

I, even I, am he that comforteth you: who art
thou, that thou shouldest be afraid of a man
that shall die, and of the son of man which shall
be made as grass; And forgettest the LORD thy
maker, that hath stretched forth the heavens,
and laid the foundations of the earth; and hast
feared continually every day because of the
fury of the oppressor, as if he were ready to
destroy? and where is the fury of the oppressor?
— ISAIAH 51:12-13

One of the things we all have to battle with is the fear of man, especially people who have authority over us and can influence our lives. How can you shake off this fear?

Firstly, what you fear is a choice. God said to Israel, "Who art thou, that thou shouldest be afraid of a man?" God went in to remind them that they had forgotten their Maker. When you choose to fear God first, there will be no room for another.

Secondly, men are vulnerable and weak. Man is described in this way, "Made as grass." Imagine an ant being afraid of another ant.

Thirdly, the power of God will protect you from the wrath of men.

God reminds us of His great power: "Stretched forth the heavens, and laid the foundations of the earth."

Finally, God assures us His power will stop the fury of any oppressor. Therefore, fear not, because God can and will preserve you!

GETTING READY FOR BATTLE

Prepare the table, watch in the watchtower, eat,
drink: arise, ye princes, and anoint the shield.
—ISAIAH 21:5

L ife is a war; from the Spirit realm to the natural,
we are always fighting something. It could be
the devil, sickness, poverty, enemies, etc. Because
of this, we must be battle ready at all times. What
are some of the spiritual preparations that we can
make?

I would like us to examine this Scripture by looking
at it symbolically.

This Scripture shows us things we can do to be
battle ready. I want us to examine them in detail.

1. **Prepare the table and eat.** This means we
   must nourish ourselves with the Word,
   which is the food of the Spirit.

2. **Drink.** We must drink "of the Spirit." Prayer
   makes you drunk in the Spirit.

3. **Watch in the watchtower**. This means we
   must be spiritually vigilant.

4. **Arise.** We must move into action.

5. **Anoint the shield.** Faith is crucial, and
   Ephesians tells us to pick up the shield of
   faith.

It's time to get ready for battle, so start preparing
yourself with these five keys!

HOW TO MANIFEST
THE POWER OF GOD

O God, thou art terrible out of thy holy places:
the God of Israel is he that giveth strength and
power unto his people. Blessed be God.

—PSALM 68:35

Do you want spiritual power and do you need it? I do, because spiritual power can help you to overcome many problems. If you do, then I want you to know that God is willing to give you power. We are told that He "giveth strength and power."

What are the conditions for obtaining this power? Let's look at a couple.

First of all, this power is available only to His people. "The God of Israel is he that giveth strength and power unto his people." You cannot have this power until you become born again.

Secondly, holiness will help you to manifest this power. This power is manifested from holy places, "Thou art terrible out of thy holy places." Terrible power or great power can be found where God finds holiness.

Being born again and walking in holiness will help you to manifest "Terrible Power." Let's do both!

HOW TO RESPOND TO A RUMOUR

And it be told thee, and thou hast heard of it,
and enquired diligently, and, behold, it be true,
and the thing certain, that such abomination
is wrought in Israel: At the mouth of two
witnesses, or three witnesses, shall he that
is worthy of death be put to death;
but at the mouth of one witness he
shall not be put to death.
— DEUTERONOMY 17:4, 6

A "rumour" is a story or statement in general circulation without confirmation or certainty as to fact. There are many people who take decisions based on rumours.

You can marry, vote, or invest based on hearsay, propaganda, adverts, or what people are saying. You may not like someone based on a rumour. You can even conclude a bad business is good based on it. You may assume someone is good when the person is bad.

Decisions based on rumours are flawed. What is the biblical response to a rumour?

Moses gave clear instructions on how to handle a rumour of idolatry against a person.

Let's examine it and glean some principles.

1. Don't draw hasty conclusions. *Enquire* or investigate the rumour.

ABOUT THE AUTHOR
KAKRA BAIDEN

Many years ago the Lord Jesus Christ appeared in a vision to Kakra Baiden and called him into the ministry as a prophet, teacher, and miracle worker. He is also known as "the walking Bible" for his supernatural ability to preach and teach the Bible from memory.

Pastor Baiden is an architect by profession and serves as a bishop of the Lighthouse Chapel International denomination. He has trained many pastors and planted many churches within the Lighthouse denomination.

Currently he is the senior pastor of the Morning Star Cathedral, Lighthouse Chapel International, Accra. He is a sought-after revivalist and conference speaker.

He is also the president of Airpower, a ministry through which he touches the world through radio and TV broadcasts, books, CDs, videos, the Internet, and international conferences dubbed "The Airpower Conference." He has ministered the Word on every continent and is also the author of the best-selling book, *Squatters*.

Pastor Baiden is married to Lady Rev. Dr. Ewuradwoa Baiden and they have four children.

For additional information on Kakra Baiden's
books and messages (CDs and DVDs),
write to any of these addresses:

US

26219 Halbrook Glen Lane
Katy, TX 77494

UK

32 Tern Road
Hampton, Hargate
Cambridgeshire
Pe78DG

GHANA

P.O. Box SK 1067
Sakumono Estates, Tema
Ghana-West Africa

E-MAIL: info@kakrabaiden.org

WEBSITE: www.kakrabaiden.org

FACEBOOK: www.facebook.com/KakraBaiden

TWITTER: www.twitter.com/ProphetKakraB

www.ingramcontent.com/pod-product-compliance
Lightning Source LLC
Chambersburg PA
CBHW060643030426
42337CB00018B/3424